Contents

Seeing the world 4

What is around my eyes? 6

What is inside my eyes? 8

How do my eyes work? 10

Why can't I see in the dark? 12

How do I see colours? 14

Why do I have two eyes? 16

What does an optician do? 18

Why do I need glasses? 20

How do my glasses help me see? 22

What if I am blind? 24

How can I take care of my eyes? 26

All about eyes 28

Glossary 30

Find out more 31

Index 32

Words that appear in the text in bold, **like this**, are explained in the glossary on page 30.

Seeing the world

You use your eyes to find out about the world around you. You are able to see huge things such as mountains and oceans, and tiny things such as beetles and grains of sand. You can detect movement and colour, as well as judge distances and positions – all thanks to your eyes.

A sense of sight

Your sense of sight is very important. Imagine trying to eat your dinner if you could not see the plate or the food on it. Imagine dressing or brushing your hair without sight.

🔍 Some people, such as the girl on the right, cannot see clearly. They must wear glasses to help them.

Inside My Body

Why do I need glasses?

Carol Ballard

www.raintreepublishers.co.uk
Visit our website to find out more information about Raintree books.

To order:

☎ Phone 0845 6044371

🖹 Fax +44 (0) 1865 312263

🖱 Email myorders@raintreepublishers.co.uk

Customers from outside the UK please telephone +44 1865 312262

Raintree is an imprint of Capstone Global Library Limited, a company incorporated in England and Wales having its registered office at 7 Pilgrim Street, London, EC4V 6LB – Registered company number: 6695582

Edited by Kate de Villiers and Vaarunika Dharmapala
Designed by Steve Mead
Illustrations by KJA-artists.com
Picture research by Mica Brancic
Originated by Capstone Global Library Ltd
Printed and bound by CTPS

ISBN 978 1 406 22098 8 (hardback)
14 13 12 11 10
10 9 8 7 6 5 4 3 2 1

ISBN 978 1 406 22110 7 (paperback)
15 14 13 12 11
10 9 8 7 6 5 4 3 2 1

British Library Cataloguing in Publication Data
Ballard, Carol.
Why do I need glasses?. -- (Inside my body)
612.8'4-dc22
A full catalogue record for this book is available from the British Library.

Acknowledgements
We would like to thank the following for permission to reproduce photographs: Alamy pp. **12** (© Stuwdamdorp), **16** (© Natural Visions/Heather Angel), **21** (© Phil Degginger), **24** (© Bob Daemmrich); Corbis p. **11** (© Visuals Unlimited); Getty Images pp. **4** (Comstock Images/Jupiterimages), **13** (National Geographic/Beverly Joubert), **18** (Blend Images/Ned Frisk), **27** (Blend Images/Ronnie Kaufman); Science Photo Library pp. **9** (Ralph Eagle), **14** (Omikron), **15** (David Nicholls), **17** (Power and Syred), **19** (Steve Allen), **25** (Will & Deni McIntyre); Shutterstock pp. **5** (Bruce MacQueen), **6** (RTimages), **10**, **22**, **23**, **29 butterfly** (© Sofia), **20**, **23**, **27 band aid** (© Isaac Marzioli), **20**, **23**, **27 gauze** (© Yurok).

Cover photograph of a boy wearing glasses reproduced with permission of Getty Images (Comstock Images).

We would like to thank David Wright for his invaluable help in the preparation of this book.

Every effort has been made to contact copyright holders of material reproduced in this book. Any omissions will be rectified in subsequent printings if notice is given to the publisher.

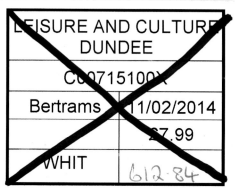

Your eyes keep you safe. Without your sight, walking along a street or crossing a road would be difficult and dangerous.

Your sense of sight can also help to entertain you. How would you watch television or read a book if you could not see? Sporting activities such as football and tennis would be impossible if you could not see the ball or the other players.

Have you ever looked closely at your eyes, or thought about how they work? Why do some people need to wear glasses but others do not?

This red-tailed hawk has sharper eyesight than any other animal.

Extreme body fact

The sharpest eyesight
A red-tailed hawk's eyesight is about eight times sharper than that of humans. This bird can spot a mouse on the ground from 1.6 kilometres (1 mile) away! A human with average eyesight would have to be closer than 200 metres (220 yards) to see the mouse!

What is around my eyes?

You have one eye on each side of your nose. The parts of your face around your eyes help to keep them clean.

Above each eye is a ridge of skin covered by a line of hairs. These are called eyebrows. They help to stop dust and sweat getting in your eyes. Around the eyes are loose flaps of skin called eyelids. Along the edge of each eyelid is another line of hairs called eyelashes. Like your eyebrows, eyelashes stop dust and dirt getting into your eyes.

Here you can see a pair of eyes with eyebrows, eyelids, and eyelashes.

Blinking helps to keep your eyes moist and clean. When you blink, your upper eyelid moves quickly down to meet your bottom eyelid. Blinking sweeps a thin layer of fluid across the eye. This cleans the eye and keeps it moist.

What happens when I cry?

Tears are the fluid that keep your eyes clean. They are made high up under your upper eyelids. They travel to your eyes through tiny tubes. Tears will usually drain away through more tubes, from your eyes to your nose.

When you cry, the tears flow so quickly that they cannot all drain away. Some spill out of your eyes and down your face. You might cry for many different reasons. You might cry because you are happy or sad, because you have hurt yourself or have been laughing a lot, or even when you give a big yawn!

SCIENCE BEHIND THE MYTH

MYTH: Cutting onions makes you cry.

SCIENCE: It's true! Onions contain a substance that irritates your eyes and makes you cry, often while you are chopping them. You can solve the problem by chilling the onion before you cut it or by holding it under water while you cut it.

What is inside my eyes?

You can see only a small part of each eye. Most of your eye is hidden and protected by the bones of your face. Each eye is round like a ball, and is often called an eyeball.

The bony ring around each eye is called an eye socket. Six muscles hold the eyeball in place in the socket. These muscles control your eye movements.

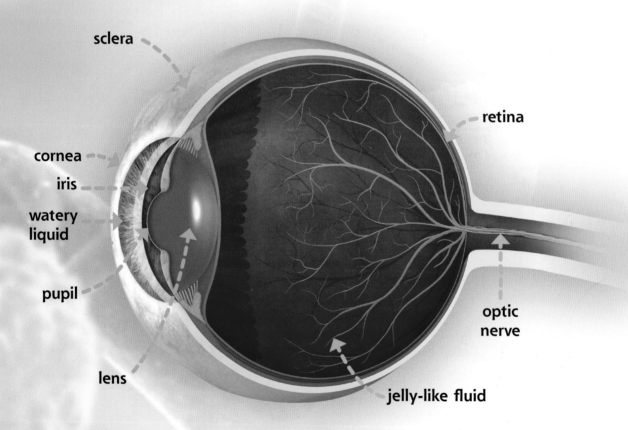

sclera

retina

cornea

iris

watery liquid

pupil

optic nerve

lens

jelly-like fluid

This diagram shows you some of the parts of an eye.

The front of the eye

The whole eyeball is covered by a tough outer layer called the **sclera**. The part of the sclera that you can see at the front of the eye is the **cornea**. The cornea is see-through. It allows light to pass into the eye.

Behind the cornea is a coloured ring of muscle called the **iris**. In the middle of this is the **pupil**. This looks like a black circle but it is really a hole that lets light into the inside of the eye. The iris controls the size of the pupil.

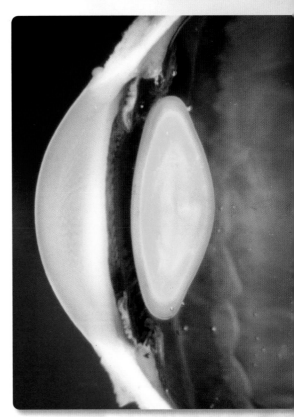

Behind the pupil is a jelly-like disc called the **lens**. This is held in place by tiny muscles which control its shape. The space between the cornea and lens is filled with watery liquid.

This is a photograph of a real eye. Compare it to the diagram on page 8. Can you find the cornea, pupil, iris, and lens?

The back of the eye

The space inside the eyeball behind the lens is filled with a soft jelly. The inside of the eyeball is covered with a thin layer called the **retina**. The retina is linked to the **optic nerve**, and the optic nerve is linked to the brain.

How do my eyes work?

Did you know that an eye is like a camera? Cameras and eyes both have a hole for light to enter and a **lens** to bend the light. They can both capture an **image**.

Light travels in straight lines from a light source, such as the Sun or a light bulb. When it hits something, it bounces off in every direction. If some of the light enters your eye, you will be able to see the object.

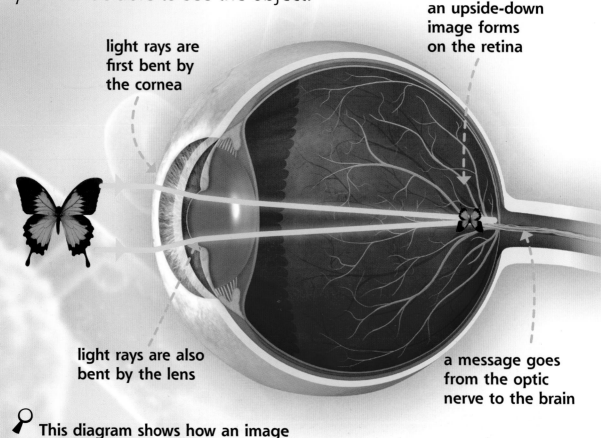

an upside-down image forms on the retina

light rays are first bent by the cornea

light rays are also bent by the lens

a message goes from the optic nerve to the brain

This diagram shows how an image is formed at the back of the eye.

How does my eye use light to help me see?

1. Light bounces off an object to your eye.

2. Light passes through the **cornea**, which bends the light a little.

3. Light passes through the lens, which bends it even more. This is important, because if the light is bent too much, or not enough, you will see only a blurry image.

4. Light travels to the back of the eye. It makes an upside-down image of the object on the **retina**.

5. The retina reacts when the light hits it, and sends a message to the **optic nerve**.

6. The optic nerve carries the message to the brain.

7. The brain makes sense of the message and you see the object.

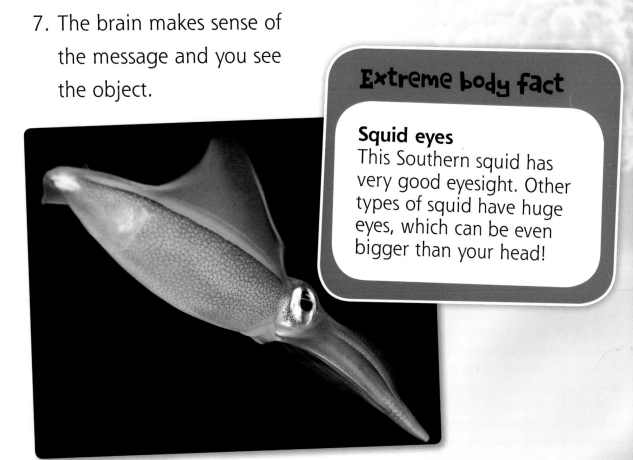

Extreme body fact

Squid eyes
This Southern squid has very good eyesight. Other types of squid have huge eyes, which can be even bigger than your head!

Why can't I see in the dark?

Look at your eyes in a mirror. How big is the **pupil**? Now shut your eyes for a couple of minutes. Look again. Does your pupil look bigger?

Bright light

In bright light, the **iris** makes the pupil smaller. This lets less light enter the eye. It helps to protect the eye from very bright light that might damage it.

🔍 In dim light (left), the pupil is large to let as much light as possible enter the eye. In bright light (right), the pupil is small to stop too much light entering the eye.

 Some animals, such as this leopard, have an extra layer behind the retina. This reflects light back into the eye. When a light shines on to the eye, the pupil seems to glow from this reflected light.

Dim light

In dim light, the iris makes the pupil bigger. This lets more light enter the eye. It helps you to see even when the light is very dim.

Your eyes do need some light to work. When it is completely dark, and there is no light at all, you cannot see anything.

SCIENCE BEHIND THE MYTH

MYTH: Eating carrots helps you to see in the dark.

SCIENCE: Yes, but only in some cases. The **retina** needs Vitamin A to work in dim light. If you are short of Vitamin A, eating carrots can help. If you already have enough Vitamin A, eating carrots will not help you see any better at all!

How do I see colours?

We can see all the colours of the rainbow. Do you know how? The **retina** plays a key part in how we see colour. It is made up of two types of very tiny building blocks called **rods** and **cones**. Rods are long and thin. Cones are short and fat.

🔍 The rods and cones of the retina send signals to the brain when light falls on them. In this picture, the rods are green and the cones are blue.

Rods and cones

Rods cannot detect the colour of light. They react to all light in the same way. Without cones, you would see everything as black, grey, and white.

There are three different types of cone. One detects red light, another detects green light, and the third detects blue light. If you look at something red, only red cones respond. If you look at something blue, only blue cones respond. If you look at something purple, some red cones and some blue cones will respond.

The brain works out the colour you are looking at from the numbers of red, blue, and green cones that respond.

Colour blindness

Some people cannot see the full range of colours that most people do. Some of their cones do not work properly. These people are said to be **colour blind**. The most common type of colour blindness is when red and green things look exactly the same colour.

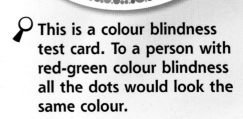

This is a colour blindness test card. To a person with red-green colour blindness all the dots would look the same colour.

Why do I have two eyes?

Hold one finger out in front of you. Shut one eye and look at it. Now quickly shut that eye and open the other one. Does it look as if your finger has jumped?

This happens because each eye gets a slightly different view of your finger. When your brain receives the signals from each eye, it puts them together. It combines the information to work out exactly where your finger is.

In humans, both eyes move together. Chameleons can move each eye separately. They can look in two different directions at the same time!

Distance, speed, and direction

Having two eyes helps you to judge distance, speed, and direction. This is really important for pouring juice into a glass, catching a ball, or stepping off a kerb. It is even more important for people such as pilots, surgeons, and drivers. These people have to be able to judge distances, speed, and directions very accurately in their work.

Compound eyes

Insects such as fruit flies have compound eyes. This means that their eyes are made up of hundreds of tiny **lenses**. Each takes a tiny snapshot view. These **images** are then put together to make up a single complete picture. This is similar to a computer screen or television screen where pictures are made up from patterns of tiny dots.

In this enlarged photograph you can see the many lenses that make up a fruit fly's eye. Hairs on the lenses help to keep them clean.

What does an optician do?

Opticians test eyes. Their results tell them how well a person can see and, if needed, they can give the person **lenses** to help him or her to see better. Their results also help them to tell whether the person's eyes are healthy.

Testing sight

One test that opticians use is a chart with letters on it. The letters at the top are bigger than the letters at the bottom. The optician asks the person to read down the chart. The better the person's eyesight, the further down they will be able to read.

🔍 **Here an optician is looking inside a boy's eyes to check everything is all right.**

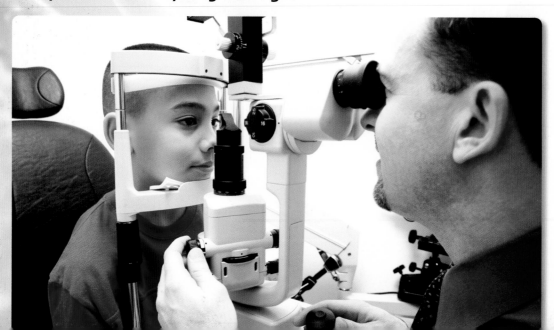

Testing health

Another test that opticians use is to shoot a puff of air at the front of the eyeball. This helps to measure the pressure inside the eyeball. The pressure reading tells the optician whether the person's eye is healthy or not.

Opticians also test eyes by shining lights into them so they can see the **retina** at the back. They look to see whether the retina is healthy or damaged.

Some opticians use a dome in which lights flash randomly one at a time over the inside of the dome. The person clicks a button each time they see a light. This tells the optician whether the person can see equally well in all directions.

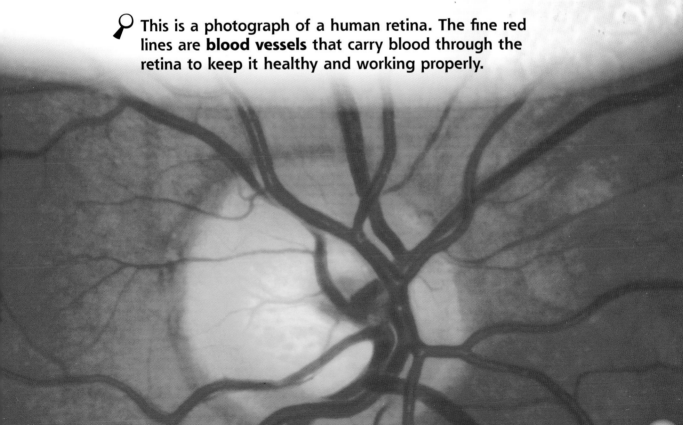

This is a photograph of a human retina. The fine red lines are **blood vessels** that carry blood through the retina to keep it healthy and working properly.

Why do I need glasses?

Do you wear glasses? Lots of people need glasses, and the chances are that either you or some of your friends or family do. Do you know why some people need to wear glasses?

Some people can see everything around them clearly. However, many other people do not have perfect vision. They wear glasses to help them to see better.

Practical advice

Wearing glasses

If you have glasses, remember to follow your **optician's** instructions about when you should wear them. Keep them in their case when you are not wearing them. Before you put them on, clean them with a soft cloth to remove dust and smudges. Visit your optician regularly.

Seeing clearly

Some people can see things that are near to them clearly, but far away things look blurred. This is called being **short-sighted**. Some people have the opposite problem: they can see far away things clearly but things close to them are blurred. This is called being **long-sighted**.

Some people see things as bent or twisted. Others see everything double. Wearing glasses can help with all of these problems.

A long-sighted person might see these clearly:
- a person standing far away
- the picture on a television screen
- the view from a window.

A short-sighted person might see these as a blur.

A short-sighted person might see these clearly:
- a person standing close by
- their dinner plate
- a packet they pick up from the supermarket shelf.

A long-sighted person might see these as a blur.

How do my glasses help me see?

If an **optician** thinks you need help with your eyesight, he or she may suggest that you wear glasses. Different types of eye problem need different types of glasses. The **lenses** in the glasses bend the light to help you see clearly.

Being short-sighted

People who are **short-sighted** cannot see things in the distance clearly. The light entering the eye is bent too much, so that it does not strike the **retina** correctly. This makes a fuzzy **image**. They need glasses with lenses that bend the light to make it strike the retina corrrectly and make a clear image.

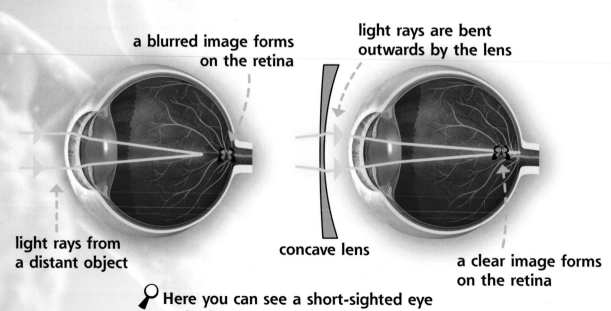

a blurred image forms
on the retina

light rays are bent
outwards by the lens

light rays from
a distant object

concave lens

a clear image forms
on the retina

🔍 Here you can see a short-sighted eye
and a lens to correct the problem.

Being long-sighted

People who are **long-sighted** cannot see things close to them. Their eyes do not bend the light enough and the light entering the eye does not strike the retina correctly. This makes a fuzzy image. They need glasses with lenses that bend the light to make it strike the retina correctly and make a clear image.

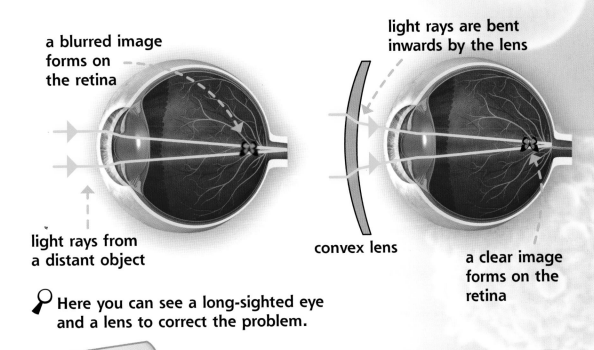

a blurred image forms on the retina

light rays are bent inwards by the lens

light rays from a distant object

convex lens

a clear image forms on the retina

🔍 Here you can see a long-sighted eye and a lens to correct the problem.

Practical advice

I hate my glasses!

If you hate wearing glasses, contact lenses may be for you. Contact lenses are tiny discs that sit on the front of the eye. These bend light just as glasses do. However, contact lenses are not suitable for everybody. Your optician will tell you whether you can wear them.

What if I am blind?

Many people are blind. Some blind people can see nothing at all. Others may be able to see some shadowy, blurred **images**, or be able to detect some movements around them.

Being blind can make everyday things, such as reading a book or watching television, very difficult or even impossible. However, modern technology can help many blind people to overcome their disability.

🔍 Blind people can use computers that have been made specially for them.

Braille

One of the earliest aids for blind people was the Braille alphabet. This uses a different pattern of dots for each letter and number. A blind person feels the dots with their fingers to reads the letters or numbers.

Getting around

Guide dogs can be trained to help blind people to get around safely. GPS (Global Positioning System) can also be used. The person holds or wears a GPS receiver which works out exactly where they are. It can give them directions to where they want to go to, and help them to avoid obstacles in their path.

$\mathcal{P}$ **A blind person can enjoy reading an exciting story that is written in Braille.**

How can I take care of my eyes?

Your eyes are very important. They are also very delicate. Here are some tips to help you look after your eyes:

- keep your eyes clean by washing your face at least twice a day

- wear ski goggles to protect your eyes from glare if you are out in the snow

- wear sunglasses to protect your eyes from bright sunshine on a sunny day

- NEVER look directly at the Sun or at an eclipse. The light is so bright it can permanently damage your eyes.

- wear eye protection for sporting activities

- if your **optician** prescribes glasses for you, make sure you follow his or her instructions about wearing them

- if you wear contact **lenses**, follow all the instructions such as how long you can wear them for, when to change them for new ones, and how to clean them.

Looking after your eyes will help them stay healthy, so you can see and enjoy the world around you.

Something in your eye?

Do not rub it, you will just make it feel worse. Instead, splash it with plenty of water to flush away whatever was causing the problem. If this does not work, you might need to see a doctor or nurse.

Alert! If you splash any chemicals in your eye, try to flush the eye clean with water and seek medical help quickly.

All about eyes

Each person has **irises** that are different from anybody else's. This means irises can be used to identify someone, just like fingerprints.

Did you know that you blink 10–15 times a minute? That is more than 10,000 blinks a day. Babies blink only about twice a minute.

Wearing coloured contact **lenses** can make you look very different. There are all sorts of colours available, from normal eye colours such as blue and brown, to amazing shades of red and yellow. Some are even patterned with flames or fur!

Unlike most parts of your body, your eyes hardly grow at all. By the time you are an adult, they will be only a few millimetres bigger than when you were born!

Parts of the eye

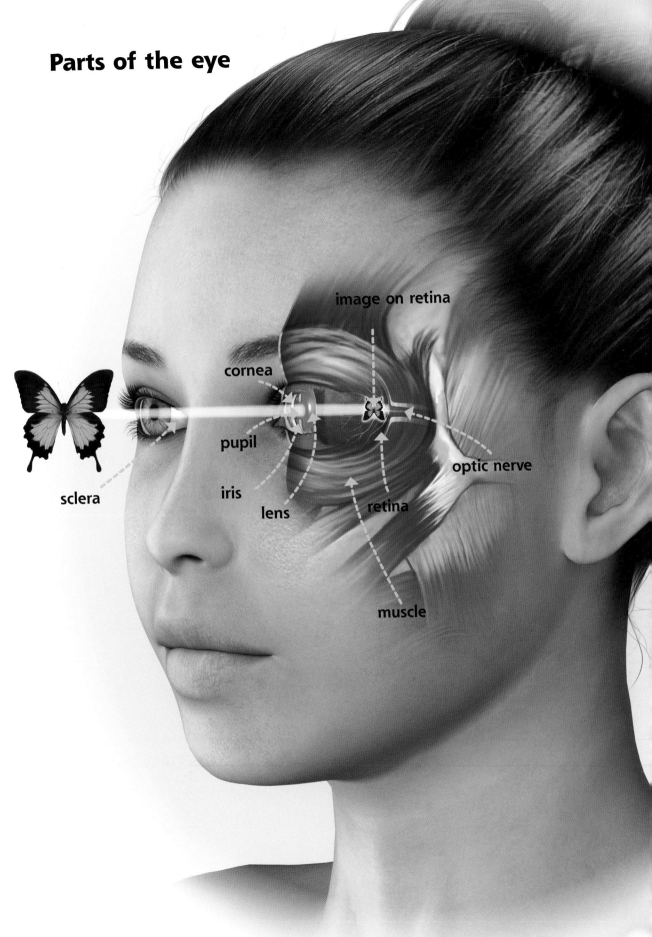

image on retina

cornea

sclera

pupil

iris

lens

retina

muscle

optic nerve

Glossary

blood vessel tube through which blood travels around the body

colour blind inability to tell some colours apart

cone part of the retina that allows you to see colours

cornea see-through layer at the front of the eye

image picture of something

iris coloured ring of muscle around the pupil

lens jelly-like disc in the eye that bends light

long-sighted to be able to see distant objects clearly but close objects less clearly

optician person who tests eyes and prescribes glasses

optic nerve part that carries messages from the retina to the brain

pupil hole at the front of the eye that lets light enter the eye

retina thin layer inside the eyeball that reacts to light

rod part of the retina that allows you to see light

sclera tough, white wall that keeps the eye in a ball shape

short-sighted to be able to see close objects clearly but distant objects less clearly

Find out more

Books

Blindness (Explaining), Lionel Bender (Franklin Watts, 2009)

Senses (Your Body: Inside and Out), Angela Royston (Franklin Watts, 2007)

The Senses (Understanding the Human Body), Carol Ballard (Wayland, 2009)

Websites

www.healthyeyes.org.uk/index.php?id=7

Discover more about eyes on this website, which also includes some fun optical illusions.

www.guidedogs.org.uk/helpus/children/

Find out all about guide dogs and how they help their owners on this website.

www.childrenfirst.nhs.uk/kids/health/body_tour/eyes.html

Take a tour around the human body on this website. See what more you can learn about your eyes.

Index

blind people
  24–25
blinking 7, 28
blood vessels 19
Braille 25
brain 9, 11,
  15, 16

colour blindness
  15
colours 14–15
contact lenses
  23, 28
cornea 8, 9,
  10, 11, 29

dark, seeing in
  the 12–13
distance, speed
  and direction,
  judging 17

eyebrows 6
eyelashes 6
eyelids 6–7
eye socket 8
eye tests 18–19

glasses 4,
  20–23, 26
GPS 25

image formation
  10, 11, 17
iris 8, 9, 12, 13, 28

lenses (eyes) 8, 9,
  10, 11, 17, 29
lenses (glasses)
  18, 22, 23
light 10, 11, 12,
  13, 15
long-sighted
  21, 23

muscles 8, 9, 29

optic nerve 8, 9,
  10, 11, 29
opticians 18–19,
  20, 22

parts of an eye
  8–9
pupil 8, 9, 12,
  13, 29

retina 8, 9, 10,
  11, 13, 14, 19,
  22, 23, 29
rods and cones
  14–15

sclera 8, 9, 29
short-sighted
  21, 22

taking care of your
  eyes 26–27
tears 7
two eyes, need for
  16–17